Moyser Road
London, SW16

Words by Martin Beaver
Photography by Alan Weller

Zolag
32 Woodnook Road
London
SW16 6TZ
MoyserRoad@furzedown.uk

ISBN 9781897633397
Copyright Martin Beaver and Alan Weller
April 2020

British Library Cataloguing in Publication Data
A CIP record for this book is available from the British Library

CONTENTS

Foreword – The Arthur Tingle project   04

Introduction   06

Furzedown

Some history   08

Wartime   14

St Paul's Church News   16

   Commercial advertising   16

   Home life   17

Moyser Road 2019

The shops   18

   Even numbers   19

   Odd numbers   40

Acknowledgements   50

Foreword

Arthur Tingle, aged 9

In November 2017, Arthur Tingle, who was then nine years old, began a project at Penwortham School. Using Furzedown's online community network, he contacted the businesses on Moyser Road and local residents in order to ask about what the shops had been in the past, and people's memories of shopping in them.

I don't know whether this was his idea, his mum's or that of his teacher. But the response was such that I thought someone should continue the project to create an updateable record of the businesses on Moyser Road.

As no-one had, during 2019 I took this upon myself and, together with local photographer Alan Weller, have contacted the people that Arthur contacted – and more. Our intention has been to record the present and enable people in the future – residents, schoolchildren, local historians, anyone – to have something to refer back to from this one year.

What we have done

The ambitions of our project are limited. I am not a historian and haven't attempted to create a history of Moyser Road, let alone of Furzedown.

We have used a limited number of sources. Some are published and are fairly readily available. Some are not, being based on face-to-face or email conversations, often via the same network that Arthur used. Where individuals' comments are quoted, their initials are included – and they are acknowledged at the end of the book.

Occasionally we employ the term 'in living memory' to record the remembrances of people who are currently alive. Memories are fallible, and while what people recall might not always be quite right, it is not necessarily wrong. They recall facts as they remember them.

Being able to revise material later is a key part of our approach, and because it is being published online as well as in book form, it can be added to or changed. This is an attempt at community history. Alan's pictures are a permanent record. But other pictures, old and new, could be included in future, and I would be disappointed if the text stayed the same for years on end. Everyone in Furzedown is welcome to add to it.

Including new content from old people before they die should be a priority. But it is no less important to know what young people experience. What is it like to be a six-year old in Furzedown in 2020? Or someone who is 15? Or middle aged?

Even at this early stage this book could easily have been twice the length that it is.

Furzedown?

The clue is in the name.
Because of the quirks of the English language, a Down is actually an upland. And Furzedown is on a plateau above the River Graveney.

Furze are gorse bushes – evergreen and spiky with yellow flowers that smell of coconut. These grow on relatively poor agricultural soil, and still feature on the Tooting Commons. They are quick growing, highly flammable and for centuries were cut by poor people, dried and burned as a fuel.

Introduction

This project is about change in a community, and is based on 20+ shops in a single street.

Change is neither good nor bad – it just happens. But faster than you think. What's more, it often isn't recognised at the time. As Joni Mitchell wrote: "You don't know what you've got till it's gone". And because memory itself is such a fallible thing, you can never be sure that what you remember was ever correct.

Most people enjoy looking at old photographs of places they know. But old photographs were new once. Alan and I have talked to almost all of the shopkeepers and business people on Moyser Road in 2019, and have taken pictures of them. What we have put together is a record of the shops in this one road in this one year. And right from the outset, we decided to take pictures in colour rather than black and white or sepia to reflect current reality rather than create art, and in a consistent style and format.

Twelve months after Arthur Tingle's inspirational request, one of the main drivers of getting this project going was the transformation of the Bradbury Pharmacy in 2018. This is the only business that has been on Moyser Road for as long as there have been shops on Moyser Road. Each version of Bradbury's – from the 1920s to the 2020s – has provided a service to the local community. What seemed sad was that there was no record of any of them, written or photographic. Perished as though they had never been.

Things continue to change. Since we started work on this project in February 2019, one shop has closed down and is currently shuttered (no 80). The premises of another business, at no 96, have been converted from a stone restoration company into apartments. And familiar faces working in shops have left.

It was a similar story in 2018 and this will, in all likelihood, be repeated in years to come.

Many people who live in Furzedown regard it as an exceptional place to live. In many ways it is.

It is also undoubtedly a community in transition. Most urban communities are and always have been.

Fifty years ago, Furzedown wasn't the way it is now. Then, for many, it was low-rent and down-market. It could also be dangerous. Running shops here has been, and sometimes is now, a risky business both physically and commercially, with the threat of robbery and cut-throat competition.

Most of the shopkeepers work exceptionally hard with long, long hours just to make a living wage.

The Furzedown community's support of local businesses is also both limited, and conditional. The area has one pub – currently called The Furzedown – that is not well regarded and is underused. In the past five years, two attempts at creating a restaurant on Moyser Road (The Village and Il Gusto) failed, in part because of a lack of local support. And in September 2019, there was an online campaign against vaping products being sold in one of the Moyser Road shops.

As in many parts of London, the older generation that bought low, is now selling high, is dying off or moving out. This means that Furzedown will continue to gentrify and change. Wealthier people will move in because of the price of houses. They will require, and doubtless support, a new range of shops and services.

In the first few days of 2020, for example, work began on converting no 95/97 from a bar that never opened into a day-care centre for dogs. It might succeed.

Remember, that 250 years ago Furzedown was the country retreat of choice for Dr Johnson and the cream of London's intelligentsia.

It might become that again – minus the country.

Furzedown Lodge is a Grade 2-listed, brick building that is currently owned by Wandsworth Council. It was built around 1840. Between 1974 and November 2019, when she died, it was the home of Glyn Bird who for many years was the head Park Keeper for Tooting Bec Common. The Lodge enabled her to live on site.

Furzedown

Imagine Furzedown as a rectangle: not quite squared off, but tilted a little to the right.

To the north it is bounded by Tooting Bec Road and Tooting Common. To the east, at one time, its border was Mitcham Lane. Now, however, that border is beyond the railway line which, mostly, separates the boroughs of Wandsworth and Lambeth. This part of Furzedown looks like the bump of a pregnancy on the rectangle.

The southern boundary follows the River Graveney along Southcroft Road – the far bank of which is the borough of Merton.

Furzedown's western edge is Rectory Lane.

The limits appear quite well defined on a road map, though the political boundaries have changed in the past and are likely to continue to do so.

Furzedown has the feel of an urban village. However, it isn't a village. It has a population of 15,500, which, if it was a separate town, would place it just outside the top 500 in the UK. And this population is divided into many neighbourhoods that are quite distinct socially and culturally, and physically relatively distant. A walk from one corner of Furzedown to its opposite, say Crowborough Road to Besley Street, is a couple of miles and might take 30 minutes depending on how young and fit you are.

But why would you do that? Furzedown exists. But it is not homogenous.

Moyser Road is, if anywhere is, the heart of Furzedown – together with Graveney School. It is central to, and accessible from, all parts of the area.

At the time of Domesday Book (1086), the whole of Tooting had a population of around 35.

Politically Furzedown is in Wandsworth. Most of it has a Streatham (SW16) postcode, and parts of the area have at one time or another been in Lambeth. However, many of the streets in the south west of Furzedown have Tooting (SW17) postcodes.

There was a time – for much of the 20th century – when living in Streatham (SW16) was regarded favourably by employers, while having a Tooting address (SW17), was frowned upon.

London postcodes were first formed in 1857. Initially Tooting and Streatham were both in S district. But in 1868 this was abolished – following a report by the novelist Anthony Trollope – and split into SE and SW. S now refers to Sheffield. (Trollope also introduced pillar boxes for the posting of letters).

The area has three shopping centres, each with a different dynamic and demographic. The most extensive, and longest established, is at the junction of Thrale Road and Mitcham Lane. There is a secondary shopping centre also to the east of Furzedown between Kettering Street and Southcroft and Fallsbrook Roads.

But Furzedown's main shopping centre is on Moyser Road which runs through the middle of the area, and this is the focus of this project.

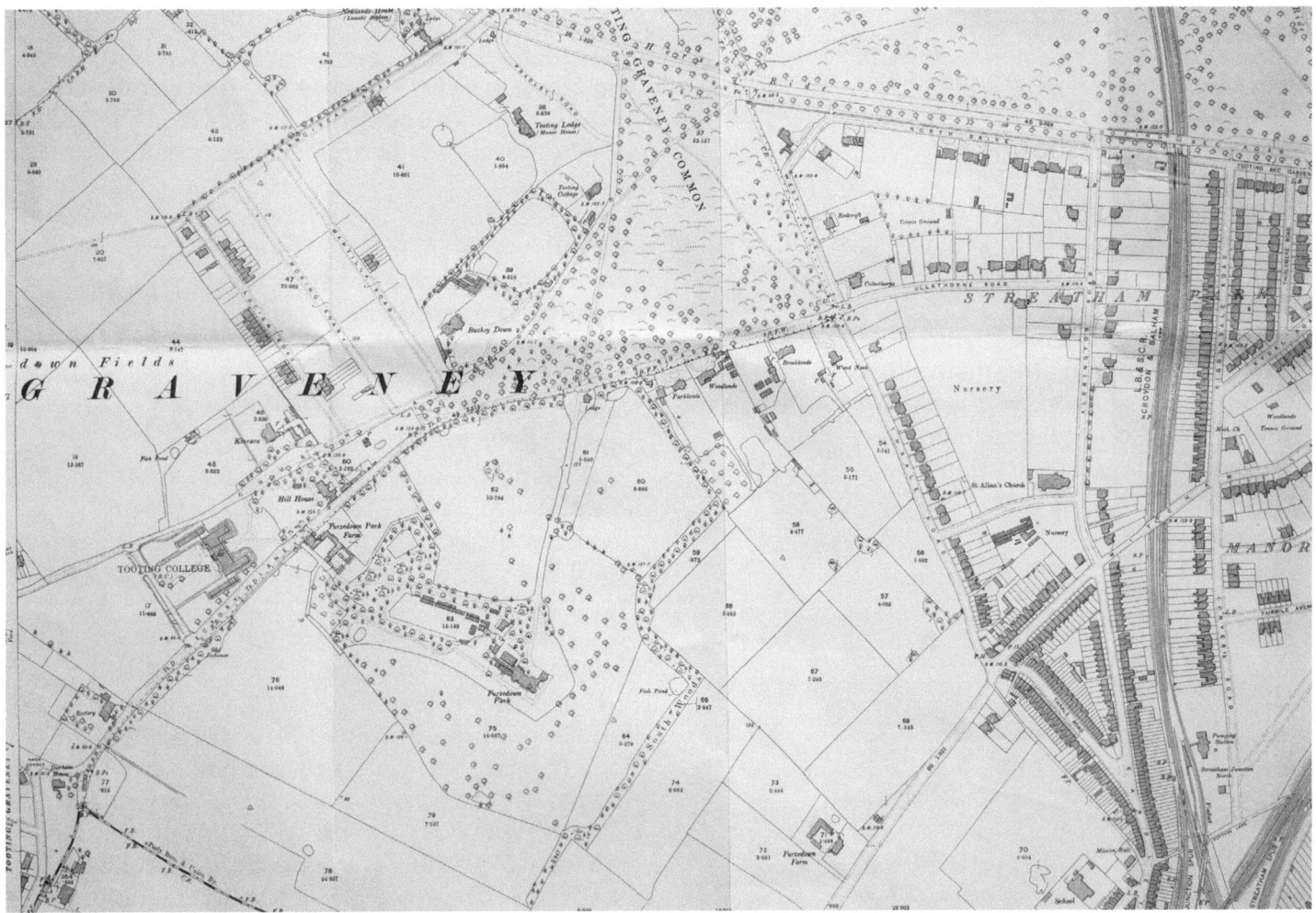

1896 – OS map – 1896 survey

1896

In 1896, Furzedown as we know it now didn't exist. Much of the space between Thrale Road and Rectory Lane was fields. There was a farm opposite what is now Dahomey Road, and the grand Furzedown Park estate with its fishpond and boundary woodland occupied approximately one quarter of the entire area. The lodge of the estate is still at the corner of Furzedown Drive. This was formerly the carriageway up to the big house, and the core of Furzedown Park house itself is now part of Graveney Upper School.

There were also four substantial houses with drives and outbuildings along the line of what is now Clairview Road. They were called Parklands, Woodlands, Brookview and Wood Nook, three of which later became road names.

However, some of today's Furzedown did exist. Eardley Road had already been built, as had what is now Goldfinch School.

Thrale Road had been laid out, and most of the large houses on the Streatham side of the road were already in place – all the way to the pub that is currently called The Furzedown. It was a public house at the time of the OS map survey. Turn the corner into Mitcham Lane, and even in 1896 there was a post office.

This closed in November 2019.

From 2003, the post office had been run by sub-postmaster Rajabali Alidina, his sister and son. Although there was no particular pressure from the Post Office to close, 70-year-old Rajabali wanted to retire and had issues with his mortgage on the building – which has now been sold. "I had hoped that the Post Office would have wanted to save it as a PO – but it is not a particularly profitable business."

1916

The 20 years between these two maps [see pages 9 and 11] show an enormous physical change – representing an even greater social change.

A fully recognisable pattern of roads has been laid out; most of the fields have been built on; and the big houses have disappeared. There is no farm and the grand house has become a Teacher Training College.

Moyser Road had been established as the main 'horizontal' (NW/SE) road through the new development. Geographically it follows the ridge-line that runs parallel to the valley of the River Graveney below – the valley that is now Southcroft Road. Many of the other roads in central Furzedown literally run up hill and down dale.

The development of what is now Furzedown began in 1901 with the laying out of Moyser, Pretoria and Pendle roads. Yet, even by 1916, only half of Moyser Road had been completed – the half from Pendle Road to Mitcham Lane. Some development had occurred towards Furzedown Drive, but it was far from complete. However, a post office had been established close to the junction with Ribblesdale Road, and the echo of that – a post box outside no 80 – still remains.

Development of the road had been completed by 1920, though some of it had to be built again as a result of the Blitz in 1940/41, and the V1 flying bomb campaign of 1944.

Moyser Road

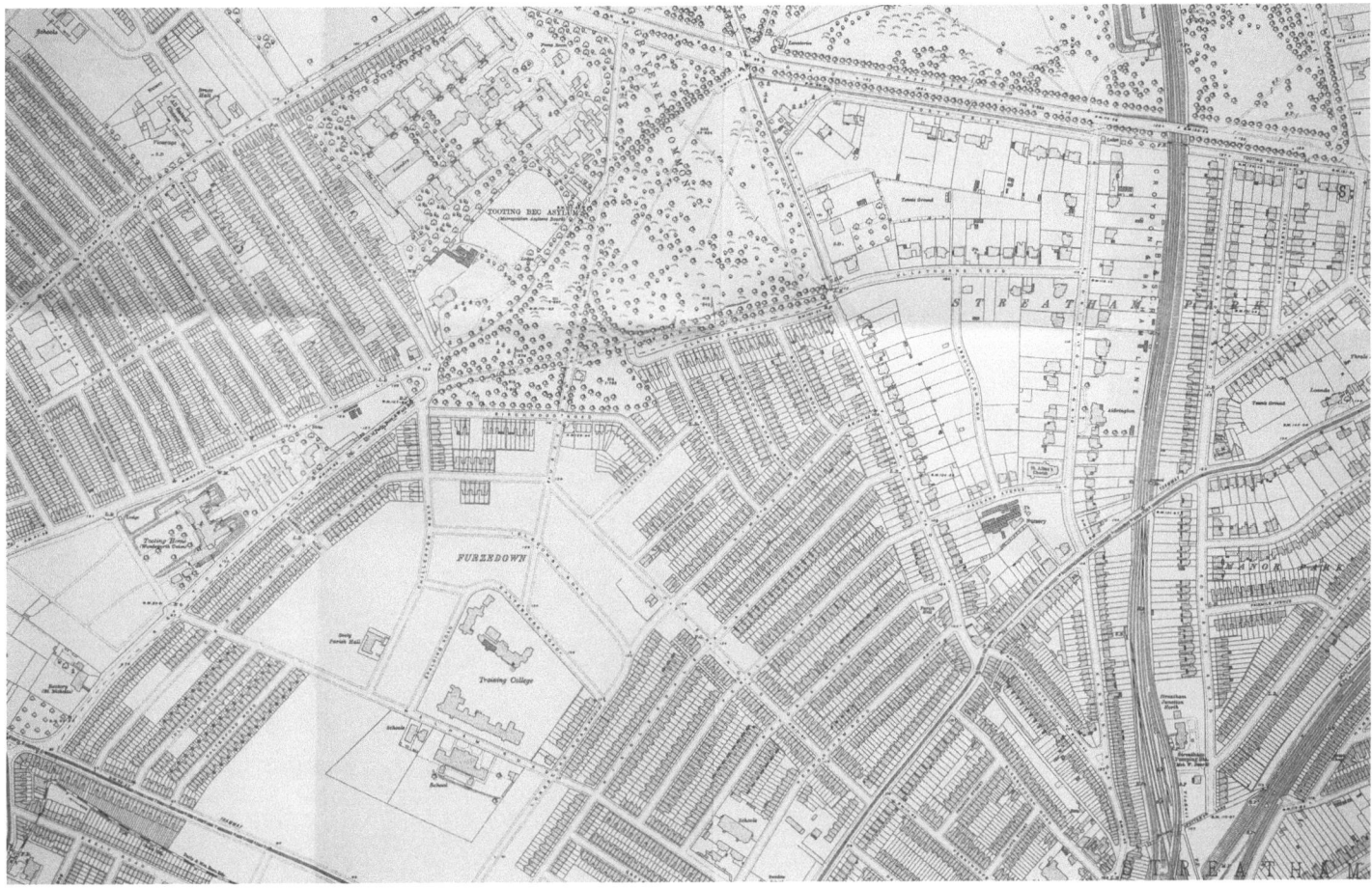

1916 – OS map – edition of 1916

1926

Transport infrastructure is of considerable importance in urban development. The southern extension of the Northern Line from Clapham Common to Morden in 1926 gave Tooting something that Streatham still lacks, and the underground continues to influence investment in and gentrification of the wider area.

The social transformation of first Clapham, then Balham, now Tooting and Colliers Wood has been inexorable as house prices have risen.

A corollary of this is that relatively poor transport has contributed to Furzedown retaining its character.

A plan, in the 1980s, to run a bus route along Moyser Road came to nothing and other than the buses along Mitcham Lane, the meandering G1 bus is the only service that currently goes through Furzedown.

The erratic route of the G1 was designed to link hospitals in the local area. St George's and Springfield are still up and running, and St John's near Clapham Junction continues as a large day hospital.

Three former hospitals – St Benedict's (between Church Lane/Rectory Lane), Tooting Bec Mental Hospital (between Church Lane/Franciscan Road) and St James' at Wandsworth Common have all been demolished and are now residential housing developments. The Bolingbroke Hospital near Northcote Road has been converted into an academy secondary school, and South London Hospital for Women and Children at Clapham South is a Tesco store and flats.

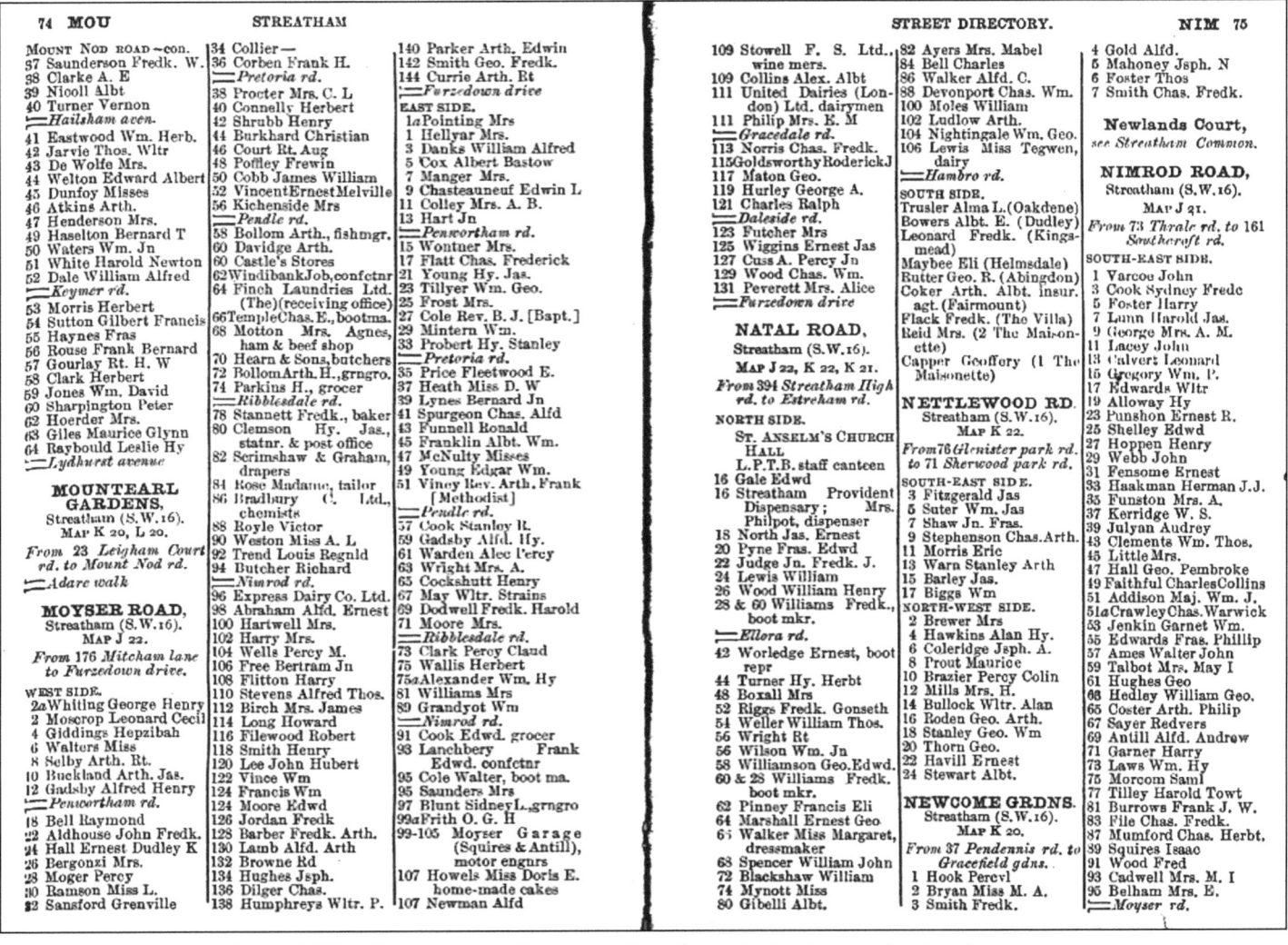

Kelly's Directories were first published in the mid 19th century. They listed the businesses in a local area.

1936 – Kelly's Directory

By 1936 all of the shops on Moyser Road were in place. These were then, and are today, at the same addresses, suggesting that they were planned that way either by the local authority or the developers – and were always a focus for the community, a key part of the infrastructure.

Individual businesses come and go and always reflect what the community needs. In 1936 the shops included two butchers, two greengrocers and a fishmonger. There was a garage, a couple of boot makers/shoe shops and three grocers.

The only shop that remains today as it was then is the pharmacy at number 86. It was called Bradbury then – and still is.

Wartime

Just one week after D-Day in June 1944, Germany launched a campaign of so-called Vengeance weapons against London – rocket-powered flying bombs. These weapons – known as V1 and V2 – were terrifying.

A disabled woman living in Penwortham Road wrote in her diary of the attack on Penrith Street on 18 June: "There is a dreadful mess the further side of Mitcham Lane, four streets without a person living in them. Every window, door and roof gone."

Less than a month later, she recorded: "All the stations are crowded with people trying to get away and crowds of children with their teachers. I get so tired of being indoors so Jim pushed my chair as far as the end of the road, the siren sounded so we hurried back to our cupboard under the stairs, ten [flying bombs] went over in five minutes but none dropped near. Last night I laid and counted 51 bangs, some near and some far away."

Wandsworth was second only to Croydon in the impact of the campaign. Furzedown suffered significantly from the V1 'Doodlebugs'. It was hit 13 times between June and August, and 39 people were killed. The worst loss of life was in Pendle Road where 12 people died when a bomb dropped between numbers 117 and 121. Five of the victims were refugees from France and Belgium – all of them women.

People were killed in Besley and Penrith Streets, in Freshwater, Southcroft and Thrale Roads – and in Moyser Road, which was hit twice.

The worst loss of life was in Pendle Road where 12 people died.

The first of these was at the corner with Furzedown Drive. This small section of Furzedown had already been attacked ten times with high explosive and incendiary bombs during the Blitz in 1940/41.

Number 140 Moyser Road – July 1944.

The second was in the middle of Moyser Road, between the junction with Penwortham and Pretoria Roads. The Incident Officer on the morning of 5 August 1944 reported not only two deaths, but also "a large crater with burst gas and water mains" and that "property was damaged over a wide area."

Moyser Road

These two pictures show the same stretch of Moyser Road – from Ribblesdale Rd to Mitcham Lane. The first is before the VI attack in 1944. The second is today. In fifty years' time, white vans and petrol cars will be as quaint as horse trams. And cones? Road markings? Phone-lines from poles?

A local woman explained what an attack meant:

"Where a bomb actually hits a house 2 or 3 others each side are also wrecked, houses opposite – or if short gardens – at the back, also are practically wrecked. Ten to 12 on either side of that and opposite will lose all windows – frames and doors and most of the plaster – and for about ¼ mile around most of the window glass goes."

Flying glass was the commonest form of injury.

The damage to houses nearby was often beyond repair. And the weather was important. If you have no roof, rain is bad. But rain also means cloud, which in turn meant that the flying bombs were less susceptible to RAF or anti-aircraft interception. Doubly bad.

The speed and sophistication of the V2s posed an even greater threat than their predecessors. But the course of the war had changed by the time they came into play. Germany was in retreat and the war was ending

The area was hit by just one V2 rocket – in November 1944. It fell on Tooting Bec Common.

* This information has been edited from the book 'Streatham's 41' published by The Streatham Society in 2019.

"My elderly neighbour was in 36 Nimrod under the kitchen table when the bomb dropped across the road in Nimrod destroying what is now 39 and 41." [SF]

St Paul's Church News

In the early afternoon of 1 July 1944, a VI rocket – a 'Doodlebug' flying bomb – destroyed numbers 34 and 36 Freshwater Road. It killed two people.

The blast damage was so extensive that the local church, St Paul's on the corner of Welham and Chillerton Roads, was unusable and it didn't re-open until June 1946.

Nonetheless, and despite the rationing of many basics – including paper – the church produced a monthly magazine. In addition to news of the Scouts and Communion, the magazine also included a wide range of articles supplied as part of the Southwark Diocesan Gazette.

Topics in the August 1946 issue included the potential impact of the atom bomb – which had been used just a year earlier, and medieval graffiti in churches.

In March 1946, there was a gag, lifted from the Roman Catholic magazine The Tablet: "Two Irish labourers, new to London traffic lights, watched the transient orange and the more enduring green. One said to the other 'They don't allow Protestants much time to get over'.

Commercial advertising

The magazine also carried adverts from local businesses that kept calm and carried on. Many of the ads provided telephone numbers: STReatham xxxx numbers. This was a time when no-one needed more than four digits, and dialling in London also required letters. However, very few people had telephones. In March 1946, barely six months after the end of the war, the magazine carried ads for Anne Swain's ladies' and children's clothing shop at 76 Moyser Road. It was also a supplier of hosiery, drapery and haberdashery, and acted as an agent for the Express Umbrella Repair Co Ltd.

Next door, at 78 Moyser Rd, R.G.Burgert (late of Harrods), described himself and his business as a high-class baker, pastrycook and confectioner – and took orders for wedding cakes. An identical ad appeared in October 1948, but under the name of R.J.Boyles.

At no 86 was C. Bradbury – Dispensing and Photographic Chemists – whose advert offered a preparation for chapped hands that was neither sticky nor greasy, alongside hot water bottles and druggists' sundries.

Number 93 was Lanchbery's newsagent and tobacconist.

In addition, Moyser Road has been, and remains, a site of commercial operations that are not part of the two parades of shops. In the 1920s for example, Percivalli, the conjuring juggler, offered magic tricks for children from 20 Moyser Road.

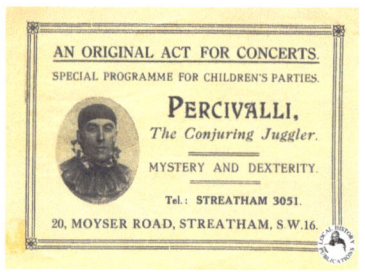

As recently as 2006, Rita Nielsen at 127 Moyser Road was advertising her aromatherapy business locally, and Alan Coles still runs Streatham Osteopaths from 114 Moyser Road.

Until the beginning of 2019 there was a stone restoration business that operated from 96 Moyser Road. During the year it was converted into a number of residential units incorporating the site's garden on Nimrod Road.

> **As a precursor of the Big Day Out, St Paul's Church held Midsummer Revels at the Church Hall in Chillerton Road in June 1949, with sideshows, stalls and a fancy-dress parade.**

> **The church currently hosts the Furzedown food bank, and in 1949 the local division of the St John Ambulance Brigade held a Medical Comforts Depot each Monday to Friday evening from 8-9pm in the Church Hall. At that time, the NHS was in its infancy and healthcare considerably more precarious.**

Home life

By 1949 the magazine hosted a page offering "WEEKDAY HINTS – For Women with Homes". These were broken down into daily tasks, such as Monday's washing. Tuesday was sewing. Other days covered nursing, cooking and household hints. Some of the suggestions would fail current health and safety rules, and some of the recipes were pretty unappealing. But the large number of suggestions were sensible and sensitive to the rationed and immediately post-war world that women faced.

In April 1949, Mrs Cook suggested using pieces of adhesive tape from parcels and packages to wind around the flex of an electric iron, especially if it was showing signs of wear and the rubber was exposed.

Mrs J Smith offered a "very nourishing idea and tasty too" with her 'Spread for kiddies bread'. This consisted of four large potatoes, mashed, and then mixed with a beef cube (like Bovril) dissolved in a little water.

June 1949 included recipes for a lotion to banish greying hair that was made from blackberry leaves and the bark of oak trees; ways to prevent small boys' pyjama trousers falling down; a remedy for whooping cough and a suggestion of using wet scissors for cutting dates or marshmallows.

It also included a recipe for Jellied Beetroot from a Mrs Paynter. This involved dicing a medium-sized cooked beetroot and covering it with a lemon jelly that had been partially made with vinegar. Mrs Paynter suggested serving it with salad. Yum.

People today don't seem to get chilblains. But Mrs Bryon's cure involved pouring a little paraffin into a saucer, dipping a piece of cut onion into it. And then gently rubbing the chilblain with the onion for at least 10 minutes, every day, for a week.

Mrs Ridsdale had devised a solution to the problem of toddlers' nappies getting out of place. She made a small pair of braces from white webbing – and it did the trick.

In November, Mrs Robson, sounding the voice of experience, recommended rubbing the wrists and arms to the elbows with Vaseline before beginning the weekly wash in winter to prevent chafing.

And Miss Mullard recommended the following: "A large mirror, hung in an invalid's room so that it reflects the garden and outside life, will provide her or him with a new interest in life."

The shops

The stretch of Moyser Road that lies between Ribblesdale and Gracedale Roads currently has 21 shops or businesses that between them employ or provide paid work for approximately 104 people full and part time. In addition, there are around 90 unpaid volunteers working at Sprout and the Furzedown Project.

There are two main parades of shops. Though barely 100m apart, they are on opposite sides of the road and are quite different in character. Human memory and the pattern of our routines means that people who may have lived in the area for 50 years can clearly remember the shops on their side of the road, but are much less confident about the others.

At the end of 2019, 14 of the 21 were small independent businesses or not-for-profit organisations, three were empty, and four were parts of chains.

Six of the commercial businesses were set up or run by white-British people. The rest were operated by entrepreneurs of EU, Turkish, Asian or African origin.

The sites are owned by a number of landlords and property companies, and all have residential properties above them, which have not been included in this project. Until relatively recently it was often a tenancy requirement that the shopkeeper lived above the premises. Some still do. Although there are several references to the rents that shopkeepers have paid in the past, current rents are also out of scope of this project.

In our research, two shops stand out in the memories of local people. These are at either end of the Moyser Road parades. The one, Peter's Fish and Chip shop, is now the Aspire estate agency. The other is the one-time launderette that is currently Café de Nero.

The Odd numbers

Of the not-for-profit businesses, The Furzedown Project (no 91/93) has remained remarkably true to its founding vision over more than 45 years.

The Evens

There are currently 15 business premises or shops on the south side of Moyser Road (the Evens side). The parade itself is divided in two by Ribblesdale Road, and all of the shops are fronted by pavement-planted trees. These trees were already in place before 1910, when the picture opposite was probably taken. They are lime trees, and today are subject to tree preservation orders.

These premises were built as retail outlets/commercial premises and are still supposed to operate as such. However one property – no 64 – has not functioned as a business for many years.

The Evens

This picture shows the shops from Aspire (left) to Sprout. Aspire, with its chequerboard tiles, was a fish shop and was promoting cod at 6d a pound. The shop next door but one, now Furzedown Cars, is advertising chocolates. A man wearing a straw boater is perhaps about to enter the shop in between, that is now Image, while at the end of the parade, another gent is peering into what is now Clarke's having parked his bicycle against a tree.

All of the shops appear to have pull-out blinds, and uniform headboards – probably glass with gilded lettering.
The pavement is raised from the road by approximately two feet (70cm), with an angled, and perhaps grassed, metre wide kerb.
There are no cars, but there was litter even then.

58 Moyser Rd

Christian Farrer has lived in Furzedown for almost 40 years.

1936 – Fishmonger
2019 – Aspire estate agency
Number of employees: 5

The profusion of estate agencies in some parts of south west London can sometimes constitute a blight.

But not in Furzedown. There are only two. Aspire, on Moyser Road, whose business looks towards Tooting and Balham (west and north west), while Barnard Marcus – on Mitcham Lane – faces east and north east to the Streatham side of Furzedown and beyond.

Christian Farrer is the assistant manager of the Moyser Road branch of Aspire. His family moved to Pendle Road from Battersea in the 1980s, and he still lives around the corner from the shop.

By the time that Aspire took over the business in approximately 2000, it was already an estate agency – trading under the name of Home London. Aspire then re-shaped the building, adding the frontage on Pendle Road, along with the flat and new-build house next door, and the patio and decking on Moyser Road, making it the most striking – and largest – of the commercial buildings in the parade.

Number 58 is a prominent corner site and has been successful for much of its life, much of which has involved fish, having been both a fishmongers and a fish and chip shop. Even now, there are marble slabs in the basement for preparing wet fish.

"Peter's sold wet fish on the mornings and fried fish in the evening." (AR)

"In the 1970s and 1980s it was named Peter's Fish Bar after its owner, a Cypriot man called Peter. People would – literally – travel for miles to buy the cod, haddock, skate, 'rock salmon' (actually dogfish), saveloys and chips that were fried there. Then it was taken over by a Chinese couple from Malaysia, who ran it successfully for many years." (PG)

"On a Friday night, the queues were half way along the parade." (EP)

"There was a fire at Peter's. It was after that that they remodelled the shop." (GG)

60 Moyser Rd

1936 – Castle's Stores
2019 – Image (hair and beauty salon)
Number of employees: 6

On 8 October 2019, Marzena Forristal posted this on the Furzedown network on behalf of Dara Pavier who owns the salon: "Last night at 10.30 someone smashed the salon door and cut the locks. Is there a handyman who could help to fix it temporarily so the salon can be locked for the night?"

The answer was yes.

A hairdresser is not an obvious target for robbery. But two young men had used a moped to ram the door. They stole just £20 from the till – and a pair of earrings left behind by a client. The initial estimate from an emergency door replacement company to repair the damage was £4,500.

Dara has run Image for three years. She bought the business from Marzena who still works there as a stylist.

This is the second time the business has been robbed in 18 months. Another unlikely target, Clarke's Florist (number 72), has also been broken into more than once.

Nonetheless, Dara, who does not live locally, seems happy with Furzedown. "I had never heard of it. But I wanted to buy a salon, and this was in budget. And it's breezy," she says, "a nice place to work." Breezy compared with Bermondsey where she also has a salon. "The staff and the clients here make life easy."

Dara Pavier – Aveda-branded hair products are key to the image of Image London.

"Image used to be a glass shop where they would cut glass and windows for you." (EP)

62 Moyser Rd

1936 – Confectioner
2019 – Furzdown Cars
Number of employees: 15

White people don't often experience racism first hand.

But even as we were talking, Nasin Sadiq, who has run Furzedown Cars since 1999, took a call in which he was racially abused and sworn at aggressively. This wasn't even a late-night drunk. It was 3 in the afternoon and the call was from someone hoping to sell mobile phones.

I was shocked, but for him it was all in a day's work.

However, that's not why Furzedown Cars is likely to close in 2020.

The reason for that is Uber and competition from other online taxi companies.

The mini-cab market has changed. Streatham-based Greyhound Cars used to be the big player locally – and probably still is. "They used to have 200 drivers. Now they have 35. We have 12."

So perhaps the business model no longer works. "I have to pay somebody to sit here for 24 hours a day [to take calls] for at least the minimum wage. Often it is me."

Nasin Sadiq

Nasin says that while parents would like to know that their children are safe, young people themselves care less. "When an Uber driver comes, you don't know who is going to turn up."

And if the mini-cab company disappears, Nasin says, it is just part of a trend. There are no longer banks or petrol stations local to Furzedown. And even the local post office has closed.

"This has been a cab office for years. In the 1980s it was run by a West Indian man, Hughie Charles, who played tenor sax upstairs.
"Hughie lived on Pendle Road and died a couple of years ago." [PG/WC]

"Mr Mills ran the sweet shop here, with big glass jars full of sweets. He lived on the corner of Moyser and Gracedale, and he had a club foot." [JR]

64 Moyser Rd

1936 – Laundry
2019 – Vacant

This has not been a shop for some years. It appears to have undergone a change of use – official or not. Although part of the shop has apparently been converted to residential, neither the flat nor the reduced retail space are currently occupied.

"At the back of this shop there used to be a lending library. It was tiny." (GG)

"When I moved in next door, number 64 was a genealogy business that specialised in researching names and surnames. This was at a time when the world wide web did not exist, and neither did personal computers so you couldn't do it yourself very easily." (AM)

Arif Malida (right) and his son Muhammed.

66 Moyser Rd

1936 – Bootmaker
2019 – A. Malida (accountants)
Number of employees: 10

Arif Malida, now in his late 60s, was born in Malawi in southern Africa at a time when it was still the British colony of Nyasaland. His grandfather had arrived there from British-ruled India around 1900 and had British citizenship.

Having graduated with a degree in economics from the University of Malawi, Arif moved to the UK in 1972, and took a Masters degree in accountancy and finance at the London School of Economics, subsequently working for one of the Big Four city accountants.

He moved to Furzedown in 1977 – he had friends here – and worked in the City until 1980 when he decided to set up his own business at 66 Moyser Road.

When he took over the premises, it had most recently been a haberdashery and sewing/knitting shop.

His clients have always been local, though they have changed considerably over the decades that the business has operated – as the population of Furzedown has changed. "One of our early clients was a pools collector." Paper football pools no longer exist, nor the need for people to collect them.

But A.Malida & Co had plenty of local tradesmen as clients – carpenters and painters. It still does, though some of the painters today are artists and the firm has a much greater number of middle-class homeworkers.

Arif's two sons, who were born in Furzedown and still live here, have taken over the running of the business.

> Haberdashers scarcely exist anymore. They sold small articles used in sewing such as needles and thread, buttons, ribbons and zips, and were vital when making and mending clothes at home was the norm. In America these items are called Notions.

68 Moyser Rd

1936 – Ham and beef shop
2019 – Cut the Mustard (café)
Number of employees: 7

Jimmy Reynoldson.

Jimmy Reynoldson has been running Cut the Mustard for five years, and named it after a phrase that his grandmother used.

He took over the shop from Juan Cardeus who had established the business as the Naked Loaf around 2012. Juan's bakery had also included number 70. That combined business was ambitious and transformed this part of the parade. But was, ultimately, unsuccessful.

Jimmy had been working as a chef in now-trendy Bethnal Green and wanted his own café – but had limited capital – just £6,000. Furzedown was cheap. Initially he cycled to the shop from East London – an hour each way. That was tough so he moved and now lives 30 metres away.

He has spent the past five years growing the business and has recently finished paying off the cost of all the kitchen equipment that sits behind the café area. And in that kitchen *"we make everything we sell – the bread, the cakes, the brunches."*

During the week he starts work at 5am and finishes around 6pm. At the weekend, which is his busiest time, he starts at 3.45am and finishes at 7. As well as all of the cooking, Jimmy employs between five and six people, has to organise staffing rotas, tax, wages and everything else that goes with running a small business.

"It's a labour of love. There are no holidays and no proper salary. I want to create a hidden gem – but one people know about!"

"In the 1990s it was called Roberts – and sold antique furniture." [AM]

Jimmy makes everything he sells in the kitchen at the back of the shop.

"My elderly neighbour who is 97 went to Penwortham School from the age of 9. She remembers the shop being a dairy with fresh milk you could buy in refillable bottles. She also used to talk about it being a bit rough round here when she first moved from Battersea 88 years ago, and that Penwortham School was particularly rough because of all the children that attended from Mitcham!" [SF]

Cut the Mustard is the only shop on Moyser Road that still has a set of decorative tiles – some of which reflect previous uses of the premises.

70 Moyser Rd

1936 – Butchers
2019 – Naked Loaf (pizzeria)
Number of employees: 3

The original Naked Loaf business, set up in 2012, occupied both number 68 and 70. It was mainly a bakery, with a little additional retail but was a step too far for the then owner, Juan Cardeus.

When Juan returned to Spain, Jimmy Reynoldson took on no 68 transforming it into Cut the Mustard, while Abramo Zingaro re-launched Naked Loaf as a pizzeria at 70.

Abramo comes from the southern Italian region of Molise but lives less than a mile from the Naked Loaf.

He is the son of a chef and has been one himself since he was 16.

Alessandro Valentino (left) is Abramo's cousin. He runs the Naked Loaf day-to-day and works with Giuseppe Serra (right).

Financial backing for setting up what he saw as "a small, community business" came from Italy. But it has been so successful that 18 months ago he was able to open another restaurant called Aubergine in Tooting Broadway, and in autumn 2019 a separate business (in Balham) supplying fresh pasta and pizza dough to other local companies.

"For years this was Hearns – a butchers. Once Hearns left, Osman took over, and it sold everything – like a pound shop. But they got robbed so many times, they stopped." (WC)

As well as flowers, Wendy Clarke also sells locally produced eggs – and always has.

72 Moyser Rd

1936 – Greengrocer
2019 – Clarkes (florist)
Number of employees: 1

Wendy Clarke has run Clarkes since January 1996 and knows more about the Moyser Road shops than almost anyone else.

"A florist makes the parade," she says. And who could disagree?

But "Floristry is a hard business to work in". The hours can be long. Sometimes she starts work at 2 or 3 in the morning and she often works 7 days a week – "People want you to be open." And three of those days she goes to Covent Garden market at 4am to buy stock. In addition, her experience has been that other people regularly try to steal your clients.

For her the business is a family thing. Her in-laws (the Clarkes) started two shops on Moyser Road in 1974 – a florist and a greengrocer – next door to one another. At that time, the same freeholder owned many of the shops on the Even side of the road.

"In 1974 the rent was £7 a week. When I took over it was £50."

Wendy still lives upstairs from the shop. That used to be a condition of the lease.

In January 1996 the greengrocery at number 74 was sold on, and then after a couple of years, closed down for several years. "That was a time when the shops and the whole area seemed to be going downhill."

It re-opened as a greengrocer – then closed again – before being reborn as Sprout.

74 Moyser Rd

1936 – Grocer
2019 – Sprout Arts
Number of employees: 0 (but 20 Trustees and regular volunteers)

Sprout Arts was set up in 2010 by Fio Adamson in a former greengrocer's shop – thus the name – that had been empty for 15 months. Opening an arts centre in Furzedown – then or now – was not an obvious thing to do. Originally conceived as a six-month pop-up, it is still going.

Fio had moved to Furzedown in 2007, and after finishing a Fine Art degree in 2009, "I was thinking art. The place had big windows, and I felt it could be a nice community art space." It also had dirt cheap rent – £50 a month – that the landlord was happy to receive as volunteers did much of the work, over 12 months, converting what was a "mess" into something new.

"We wanted to show the stained glass in the windows, the hooks in the ceiling, and to put on events, including workshops and music." Workshops still take place. But people live upstairs so events are more muted.

"We originally encouraged local young people to spray paint the shutters. But there was feedback about this and fear that house prices would go down."

Fio Adamson.

Fio is no longer closely involved with Sprout, though Lynn Selwyn-Reeves is. She is another local artist – a photographer.

"Sprout is still run by volunteers," Lynn says, and it is still a not-for-profit set-up. Now, however, it is more of a gallery than an arts centre. "Exhibitions change every two weeks and there is more demand from artists than time-slots available."

Shows are mainly, though not solely, of work by local artists. They pay an exhibition booking fee, and a commission on sales to Sprout which, along with income from card sales and revenue from memberships, pays the rent and bills.

"It is nice to have something as airy fairy as Sprout, that is not all about the money," Lynn says. But while Sprout was initially based on goodwill, she says it now needs to be somewhat more professional. So in 2020, Sprout plans to have a proper programme of workshops.

The shop with no name.

76 Moyser Rd

1936 – ?
2019 – Property developer
Number of employees: 3

This business is an enigma.

Number 76 doesn't even appear in the 1936 Kelly Directory which skips from number 74 to 78 without missing a beat. Even today there is no name, no signage, and tinted windows.

The pavement outside of the building – crazy slabbing with brick patterns – is the only one of Moyser Road's even numbers not to be fronted by tarmac – except for the raised deck at 58. It has glass bricks in the skirting wall allowing light into the basement. It's like MI5, hiding in plain sight.

But if the company doesn't need to promote itself, why would it?

It is a property development business. It has been run from here by Tahir Ahmed since 2000. Three people work in the office, excluding Mr Ahmed. He buys properties, develops them and lets them out. He owns number 76 and other (non-commercial) buildings in Moyser Road.

His business operates over a relatively wide but local area: in Brixton, Balham and Streatham, where its main office is located.

"The office on the corner of Ribblesdale Road used to be a grocers – the Commonwealth Stores." [EP/PG]

"This was a haberdashers, more than 60 years ago, run by Miss Cummings. I can still picture her. It was my favourite shop with its colours and silks. When I was two weeks old my mother left me outside the shop. It was only when she got home from shopping that she realised she had forgotten something." [JR}

Moyser Road

This photograph, taken c1908, shows four of the six shops that sit between Ribblesdale and Nimrod Roads.

It is likely that the picture was taken quite soon after the shops were built. Only two of them have lights outside (probably gas powered), and the six trees in front of them are stick thin. All of the trees are still there, though any evidence of the lights has disappeared.

Number 76 was a Hosier's and Fancy Draper's, the corner entrance of which faced Ribblesdale Road – as it still does. No 78 (now Kaptan) was a Baker and Confectioner operating under the unusual (and possibly German) name of G. Rehm. This was the only one of these four shop buildings to have decorative tiles as part of its fascia. Although the current frontage is almost entirely glass, very similar lotus-flower tiles survive on the exterior of No.68 (Cut the Mustard).

In 1908, no 80 was called Thrift, which is more likely to be a family name than an Edwardian equivalent of Poundland. It proclaims itself to be a post office on the window, on a small hanging sign and the headboard of the shop – which also says it was a savings bank as well as a fancy goods and stationery business. Small post offices continue to provide similar services today.

Number 82 (now Emrah) was still vacant but about to become the Don Tailoring Co offering ladies' and gents' outfits at popular prices.

Erdogan – the dapper chap.

78 Moyser Rd

1936 – Baker
2019 – Kaptan (dry cleaner)
Number of employees: 1

The man who runs Kaptan is called Erdogan – the same name as that of the Turkish president. He himself is a Turkish Cypriot.

"I've run this place for nearly 20 years.

"It was already a dry-cleaning business when I bought it, in 2000, and the man I bought it from was called Kaptan. He was Turkish Cypriot too, and sold it in order to open Café de Niro."

Erdogan trained as an electrician in Cyprus. His wife is also Turkish Cypriot, though British born. When he came to the UK, his mother-in-law got him a job at her neighbour's dry-cleaning business. "For a month I worked there for free, learning what to do. Then for the next year and a half, I was paid. After that I worked at another cleaner for 18 months before buying my own business."

According to Erdogan, there is a tradition among both Greek and Turkish Cypriots of operating dry-cleaning businesses. "Though that's changing. Increasingly shops are being run by Pakistanis."

But a bigger threat is from the internet. He says that most local dry cleaners are facing pressure from centralised operations that use firms such as Uber to collect and return cleaning for time-poor customers.

His own clientele has changed. "There are fewer families than there used to be," he says, "and more younger, single people. People who might otherwise have lived in Clapham or Balham – but moved to Furzedown because it was cheaper."

"The dry cleaners used to be a butchers. Then it was a West Indian bakery (if I'm not wrong) before it became the dry cleaners." [EP]

Erdogan does repairs as well as cleaning.

80 Moyser Rd

1936 – Stationer and post office
2019 – Mini-market

21 June 2019
The Kumars were closing down.
Neither he nor his wife wanted their picture taken.
Why would they?
The shelves were threadbare, increasingly empty as the stock was sold off cheap till the shutters fell for the last time.

The couple were collecting the post, reading the meters, checking the security. They had bought the shop 10 years earlier. Over that time there had been tenants, enthusiasm, investment and change. But it all came to nothing.

"There is no support now," Mr Kumar said. He sounded both wistful and angry. The Kumars know that eventually someone will see this shop as an opportunity. At some point it will be something else. But who knows what or when?

Until 2005 the site was a Post Office and had been for almost a century. It was a focal point on the road that was itself a focus for the community.
The Post Office was run for many years by Pat and Roy Holden, and then from 1989 until 2001 by Jay Patel. She now works in Nettles Pharmacy at the corner of Noyna Road and Tooting High St.
"Furrzedown was a nice little village, but we hadn't had a break for 7 years, working 6-7 days a week," which is why she sold it on.
Once the Post Office closed, it was no more than a mini-market, and Moyser Road already had a couple of other grocers that were bigger and better.

Not until we photographed the shop did I notice the mis-spelling.

"It was a newsagent with a Post Office at the back. But they used to sell toys, and not just board games. There were toys as big as bicycles hanging from the ceiling." [JR]

"There was a cigarette vending machine outside" (MMal)
Cigarettes, which today you can only buy from behind shutters, were available until relatively recently in packs of 20, 10, 5 – or even individually from small traders – with few if any controls.

Besides which they were available to anyone, of any age, at any time, from vending machines placed outside shops. All you needed to buy them was the right small change. Cigarette machines were a standard item of street furniture – though vulnerable to robbery.

All cigarette machines – including those in pubs – were banned in 2011.

Moyser Road is in the hinterland of Cynthia Payne's notorious Ambleside Avenue establishment. "In the early 1990s, there was also a scandal, published in the News of the World, about the Moyser Road postmaster, an illicit relationship, and ring doughnuts!" (JM)

Emrah Piro has spent her life in and around the shop. "Some clients have known me since I was baby."

82 Moyser Rd

1936 – Draper
2019 – Emrah (hairdresser)
Number of employees: 6

"Our hairdressers, Emrah, has been here for 38 years. The ground floor of this building used to be a haberdashery shop before we had it and there was a hairdressing salon based above it. That later moved down stairs and a couple of years after that my parents bought it."

Emrah's father, Mehmet, actually bought the salon while his wife was in hospital having given birth to Emrah. And named it after his new daughter. It was a surprise. But was it a treat?

It certainly changed their lives.

"Mum and dad successfully built the business up and 10 years into the business they branched out and bought two other salons – in Mitcham and Croydon. A family member took over at Moyser Road for six years while we branched out.

"In 1996 I left school and as my lifelong passion was hairdressing, I naturally came into the family business. That was when my mum and I came back to run Moyser Road.

"We had all three salons for 20 years. My dad decided about 12 years ago to sell the other salons and semi-retire. He now works with us back in Moyser Road."

The family are Turkish Cypriots. Mehmet's brother ran a dry-cleaning business on Mitcham Lane in the mid-1970s. Emrah, who is now 39, lived above the shop till she was five and has worked in it for 23 years.

"Out the back there used to be a small factory that made prosthetic limbs. It closed about 1997." [EP]

84 Moyser Rd

1936 – Tailor
2019 – Cunningham of London (wood-burning stoves)
Number of employees: 2

There are few things more homely than a wood-burning stove.

The Cunningham business is owned by Maxwell Cousins who took over from a similar stoves business called Hannings, in 2017. That had been established by Marzena Forristal, who was also responsible for opening the Image salon at no 60. The Cunningham name is that of Maxwell's grandparents.

The shop is a showroom and office, and is run on a day-to-day basis by Kayleigh Sam-Smith. She lives in Finchley, and on four evenings a week attends university in central London where she is studying for a business degree.

She says that Cunningham has plenty of local customers – "There are lots of owned houses in Furzedown – people walk past, and come in – and there are not many local fire/fireplace suppliers". Plus, she says, there is still free parking on Moyser Road which is important.

The fact that the London Assembly and Mayor Sadiq Khan are imposing restrictions on wood-burners will not be a game-changer for Cunningham, as they also sell electric and multi-fuel stoves.

Kayleigh Sam-Smith

....

Roger Griffiths is unusual. He is a vociferous Furzedown Conservative.

Between 2010 and 2014 he ran Furzedown Furnishings from no 84, taking over from a children's clothes shop called Deb Deb. His rent was £125 a week. Furzedown Furnishings was, primarily, a curtaining business. Its manufacturing was in Bickersteth Rd in Tooting, and no 84 was its showroom.

But "footfall is vital," he says, and without it "the only way a business along here will flourish is via a web presence."

Once his lease ran out, he moved his retail and manufacturing operations to Balham's Heaver Estate where rents were much higher but opportunities greater.

"This used to be a shop that repaired electrical goods like washing machines and hoovers." [EP]

Ermelinda Rende

86 Moyser Rd

1936 – Chemist (Bradbury)
2019 – Chemist (Bradbury)
Number of employees: 6

For a hundred years, only one shop has been a fixture on Moyser Road – C Bradbury, the chemist.

In that time, the business has had just four owners: the original Mr Bradbury; a Mr and Mrs Scott, who ran Bradbury's for more than 30 years before selling it to Bhavish Patel. He in turn was the local chemist for 33 years until the Pearl Group bought the pharmacy in 2017.

Since December 2018, the manager has been Ermelinda Rende.

Ermelinda is 31 years old. She is from Calabria in southern Italy. Her father is Italian (and a doctor), her mother was born in Uganda.

She trained as a pharmacist in Italy, moved to London in 2015 and before taking over at Bradbury had been working at another of Pearl's 14 pharmacies – Barrons in Tooting High St. She began working on the counter, learning how to run a pharmacy from the bottom up, and says of Bradbury's: "This is my baby. And I love to leave something of myself wherever I work."

Pearl invested a considerable amount in its transformation of Bradbury's from a rather higgledy-piggledy shop that was closer to the 1950s than to the 21st century, into a bright, open space. It now has its own consulting room in which the pharmacist – Ermelinda – can provide NHS services that were not previously available in Furzedown.

"When the Scotts had it, it was like a Victorian apothecary, and they had scales to weigh babies. In Mr Patel's day, a local schizophrenic man stabbed his father in the shop. The father was taken away by air ambulance." [JR]

Julie Kattenhorn, 64, has worked at Bradbury's since 1997, though she moved to Furzedown three years before that.

"When I moved here there were two doctors' surgeries on Thrale Road and a Post Office just along from the chemist. So people, even elderly people, could bring in their prescriptions when they were using the other local services.

"The area is more up-market now, and Pearl reflects that. People buy different things."

Bradbury's offers many services – including PRESCRIPTIONS & ADVICE. On top of the green neon letters behind the counter are small wooden signs that offer advice such as "All you need is love, and a glass of wine."

....

Until 2018, for most people who live in Furzedown, Bradbury's was Mr Patel – Bhavish – who took over the shop in 1983.

"I had been trained as a community pharmacist and that is what I wanted to be. And I wanted to have a business of my own. Number 86 was always small. But I couldn't afford to buy anything bigger. I was always happy with what I had, and refurbished it in 1986.
"When I took it over, the two shops – 84 and 86 – were double fronted and the door was in between the two. We changed that in 1986. Number 84 has been many things since – an office, a washing machine repair shop, a children's clothes shop.

"I owned the Bradbury business, but I never owned the property. That was always leased. And I didn't want to sub-let upstairs to tenants. It always felt like it would be too much hassle – and I paid higher council tax in order not to have upstairs occupied. When I bought the business, the freeholder owned five or six properties in the parade. But she has sold all but two of them.

"Bradbury's earned me a living. I thoroughly enjoyed the people of Furzedown, the community feel and being able to talk to people. Furzedown felt like a village – yet five miles from here, no-one would have heard of it! But it has become a lot more affluent over the past decade, and there are more young people. The schools are important.

"I was very much a traditionalist, and when I left had been there for 33 years. I had seen couples arrive, have children and watched them grow up. Over the years the counter trade diminished – it moved to the supermarkets. And the reputation of pharmacists was undermined by successive governments.

"By the time Pearl took over the shop was certainly due for another makeover. It had become outdated and they were right to renovate it completely."

Bhavish Patel and his wife at his retirement, as they left Bradbury's for the last time.

96 Moyser Rd

1936 – Express Dairy
2019 – Residential

Though not part of either parade of shops, no 96 was for a long time a commercial operation.

Until late in 2018 this site had most recently been a stone restoration business. But during 2019 it was converted into a number of apartments that extend into the former garden of the site along Nimrod Road.

In the 1930s it had been a branch of Express Dairy but it has been many things since – including a garden supply shop and an ironmongers.

"In the 1970s this was a children's clothes shop. I bought my daughters' clothes from there." [PG]

114 Moyser Rd

1936 – Private house
2019 – Streatham Osteopaths
Number of employees: 7

114 Moyser Road isn't actually a shop, and it never has been. It isn't in Streatham either, though it trades as Streatham Osteopaths.

It is one of the many small businesses that, over many decades, have operated within Furzedown from private houses.

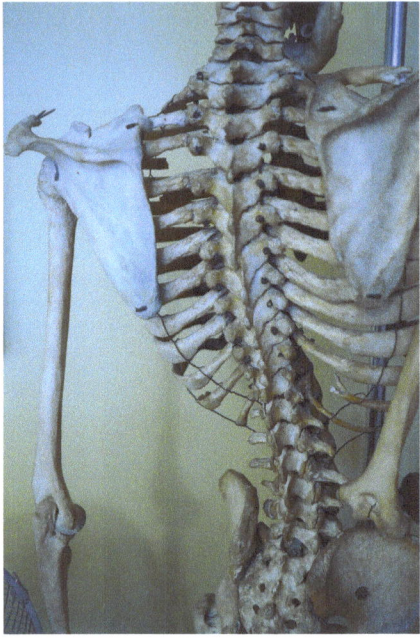

Until the advent of group practices towards the end of the 20th century, many GPs used to work from home.

Not that this is a new business. Alan Coles, who currently runs Streatham Osteopaths, took over the practice in 2002. It overlooks Café de Niro, which at that time was vacant – though still bearing the signs of its former life as a launderette.

He was also one of the people who responded to Arthur Tingle's call in 2017, saying that the osteopath business had been at 114 since 1987.

Alan bought what was an already well-established practice, and it has subsequently thrived. There are currently four osteopaths working there, as well as a specialist in Chinese medicine and two massage specialists.

Osteopathy is a complementary, as distinct from an alternative form of treatment, that is widely used for back problems. Much of his work tends to be outside of the NHS, in part because "GPs don't always know how to refer to us."

Increasingly the internet is impacting his business. "Now, 45 per cent of all new patients come via the internet. The rest continue to be by word of mouth."

Alan Coles is a specialist in sports injuries, having studied sports science at university and played squash as a professional.

He undertakes regular – and challenging – fund-raising adventures on behalf of the Furzedown Project.

In November 2019, this involved trekking up to Everest base camp in Nepal, 17,600 ft (5,400m) above sea level. In previous years he has cycled over the Pyrenees, and two years ago was in Chile tackling Aconcagua, which is the highest mountain in South America.

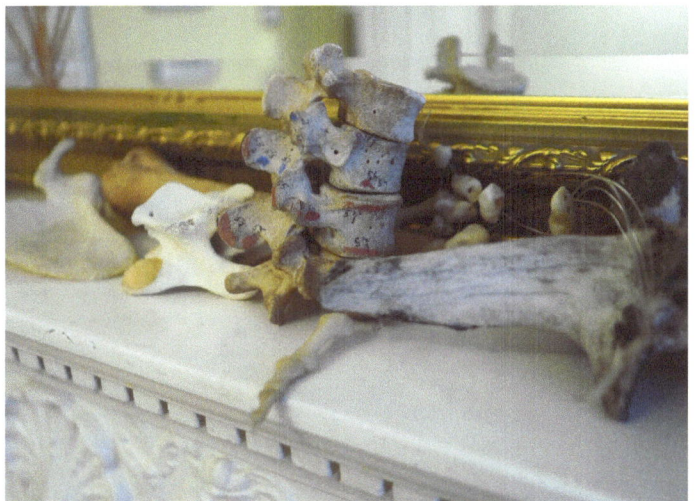

As well as a full human skeleton hanging in his consulting room, Alan has a collection of vertebrae on his mantle shelf. Some are human, some are huge and some are fossilised. Others range from coyotes to boa constrictors.

The Odds

The odd-number sites from 91 to 111 Moyser Road have always been commercial premises. However, unlike the even numbers, they have almost all morphed into double-fronted units rather than remaining as single frontages. The only exception is no 111 which is currently Café de Niro.

Also unlike the evens, these shops have had no trees in front of them – until 2019. On 16 December three trees were planted. Nonetheless these shops retain an exceptionally wide pavement in front of them with parking bays for cars and locking places for bicycles.

Planting trees in urban environments is complicated. While the lime trees on the Evens side of Moyser Road are almost a century old and are protected by preservation orders, the new trees on the Odds have to fit into an existing subterranean infrastructure of cables and pipes that we all rely on – water, gas, electricity and telecoms.

The profusion of utilities has meant that instead of four trees, only three have been planted. Two of these are Catalpa – or Indian Bean Trees. The middle one is a Liquidambar, or Sweet Gum. Both originate from the south east of the United States.

91-93 Moyser Rd

1936 – Grocer (91) and Confectioner (93)
2019 – Furzedown Project
Number of employees: 6

Look at the signage.

In the early 1970s, the sign that currently says 'The Furzedown' used to be a tyre shop. The sign that says 'Project' was a tile shop.

The corner site (no 91) has been many things – including a small Co-op store. But in 1975 it became home to The Furzedown Project – the creation of a local GP, Dr Norman Levinson, who had run the Greyswood practice (that has now shifted to Eastwood Street).

"Early in 1973 there occurred an event, which made me aware of the great danger of isolation in the elderly," Dr Levinson wrote. "A couple were found in their house having died probably 24 hours earlier. The husband was a double leg amputee, a war casualty and had been looked after by his wife. They had become rather reclusive and had cut themselves off from their neighbours. In time neighbours assumed that no help was welcome, and so they were left to cope by themselves."

The old couple had died of flu. But the doctor felt that "this kind of situation should not have arisen." So he did something about it. And the result is The Furzedown Project.

Mick Morrell (centre) has been the manager of The Furzedown Project for 12 years. Clive Brown (rear) is responsible for the home visiting aspect of the Project's work, and Pauline Copas is the Project Co-ordinator.

The original concept of The Project was to:
- *be open Mondays to Fridays*
- *stimulate community care and encourage self-help among older people*
- *and to use local skills possibly made redundant by retirement.*

"The Furzedown Project is a three-legged stool," says manager Mick Morrell. "It provides activities at The Project, home visits for the housebound, and a mini-bus service to the centre to enable people to participate. We get 220-230 visitors in a typical week."

The Project has two full-time members of staff and four part-timers, but relies on a workforce of around 70 volunteers. Some funding is from Wandsworth Council, though annual membership fees (there are 450 members), activity fees (normally £2) and room hire also contribute. And The Project has received a substantial grant from the developers of Battersea Power Station.

Number 91 was once a small Co-op. Part of Dr Levinson's intention for The Project was "to set up a kind of buying co-operative where we could buy foodstuffs at economical prices and especially cater for those living alone." While local retail options have increased over recent decades, The Project still operates a shop each Wednesday.

Dr Levinson

Change in process – January 2020.

95-97 Moyser Rd

1936 – Bootmaker (95) and Greengrocer (97)
2019 – Moyser Bar (unopened)

Until approximately 2010, this site was two separate shops. The one (no 95, next to The Furzedown Project) was a bookmaker, and the other a shop that appeared to store or repair, rather than sell, electrical goods, and that was never open.

Since the two units were merged, it has operated as a Lebanese/Turkish restaurant called The Village, which closed after two+ years, and then, after a refurbishment, re-opened as Il Gusto, a restaurant serving Italian-style food. This was even less successful, closing in late 2017. While notices on the site have subsequently suggested it might open as The Moyser Bar, it has remained closed.

2019:
- In April, I spoke to the owner who said that he was proposing converting it into a drive-through car wash.
- In October a notice, briefly, appeared in the window stating that the landlord was repossessing the property.
- On 16 November bailiffs arrived together with two white vans from an auction company based in Hull. They took away all of the kitchen equipment, while some of the furnishings and small electrical items were taken by the owners of Café de Niro.

"Before it was the electrical shop, no 97 was a driving school. The bookies on the right-hand side (no 95) also sold Foster's and cider – though legally you can't have a licence for both gambling and booze." (JM)

"Until the first decade of this century, no 97 used to be a garage, where the car mechanics were a man and his wife." (PG)

Suraj Shrestha (left) with supervisor Rikesh Maharjan.

99-105 Moyser Rd

1936 – Moyser Garage (motor engineers)
2019 – Budgens
Number of employees: 15

The building that currently includes Budgens is relatively new. It is a 1960s construction set between buildings from the 1920s.

Unlike many such in-builds in London, and even in Furzedown, this wasn't a bomb site. It used to be a garage, that at one time was owned by Godfrey's – perhaps linked to a local Ford dealership or the Godfrey and Gillman funeral directors in Balham.

Budgens is not only a shop, but has always been linked to accommodation above it and in the next street. According to Wandsworth Council's Planning Department an application was agreed in December 1962 for the "the erection of four shops and four maisonettes on the Moyser Road frontage and 2 two-storey houses on the Gracedale Road frontage with an access from Nimrod Road."

A subsequent application, in August 1967, was for "the erection of a supermarket with four self-contained flats."

Being the largest supermarket within walking distance of any part of Furzedown, Budgens is at the heart of the community. The shop is a franchise, and the franchisees are Suraj Shrestha and Noor Warsama. Suraj is from Nepal, and Noor has Somali roots.

While Suraj clearly loves Nepal, he came to England as a student in 1999 "and you get sucked in".

Having completed his Masters degree in business management, he and Noor took on the franchise in 2006. "At that point the store wasn't up to scratch. But we worked really hard, and me and Noor are not scared to try things. If they fail, they fail."

Although today the Budgens brand is ultimately owned by Tesco, franchisees are able to stock what they want and source products from suppliers they choose. For a shop of its size, Budgens Moyser Road offers a surprisingly wide range of products, from coal and kindling to vegan ready meals, kombucha bottled in Australia and jams made in Nimrod Road. "Actually it's sad that there aren't more local products."

The range changes to reflect customer demand and changing demographics. "Furzedown is a unique environment," Suraj says, "not Tooting, not Streatham. It's a small village. People talk to each other on the street, and keep in touch through the online network."

Graveney School is also important for Budgens – not only for lunchtime meal deals for pupils during term-time, but for the parents it attracts to the area.

And Suraj is happy that Nisa is next door. "It's good that there is competition. It provides customers with options. If we were a monopoly here that would be bad. It would imply that we are expensive – which we aren't."

"Budgens has been a large frontage supermarket for the 35+ years I've lived around the corner in Nimrod Rd. It's a bit confusing because it was a Costcutter which became Budgens and the two small shops next door joined together to become a Costcutter which has morphed into Nisa! Old Bill Eldridge, long since passed away, moved to Nimrod in 1942. He told me that there used to be a garage where Budgens is now – and he worked there driving a lorry." [MM]

"Where Budgens is now has had various names. It was the International Stores in the late 1970s and then Shopper's Paradise – a shop where only some goods were put out on the shelves and you often had to pick products out of the boxes that were spread around the floor." [PG]

"Godfrey's lorries used to carry away building rubble – instead of skips that we use today. They never carried new stuff." [JR]

Most of the staff in the shop have Nepali or Sri Lankan backgrounds. One obvious exception is Ghanaian-born Paapa Ellington.

He came to London in 2002, from Sweden where he was naturalised and had studied geology.

He is also a fundraiser. "As a Christian I give 10% of my income to charity."

One spectacular success has been his sponsorship of a young Nepali girl. Paapa didn't even know her – though Suraj did. Paapa sponsored her training as a nurse in Nepal, and subsequent Masters degree in the US. She is now contemplating doing a PhD.

In May 2019, she came to the shop. "That was the first time I had met her. It was very emotional. If I help her, she can help many other people. She is becoming a leader.

"I'm from Africa. I've been supporting people not from my country and not of my race. That helps people to see that they can do that too.

"When I was a child," he says, "I used to have to walk five miles to change books in the library. Furzedown has people who know that books can change lives." And collaborating with Graveney School, Paapa sends books to three schools in Ghana. So far he reckons he has sent 20,000. The shipping cost is paid, in part, by the blue pot on the counter near the tills. That generates about £30 a month.

His fundraising focuses on skills, apprenticeships and entrepreneurship. "I try to help people in Ghana manage their resources better, and when I go back I explain how to prepare to make use of the opportunities in Europe.

Paapa Ellington

"I encourage young people in Ghana to work on the land, rather than moving to the city. I encourage them to set up businesses growing vegetables." He sends seeds to Ghana where the environment and climate means that a relatively high value product such as tender-stem broccoli can produce four crops in a year.

And in action against climate change he is encouraging the planting of coconuts – which remove carbon dioxide and provide food.

107-109 Moyser Rd

1936 – Home-made cakes
2019 – Nisa Local
Number of employees: 7

The fact that Budgens and Nisa are next door to one another is not unusual: there has always been a profusion of grocery shops on Moyser Road. People need them.

Like Budgens, Nisa is a franchise (and it is pronounced 'nicer' rather than 'neesa'). It is part of the Co-op group, which explains some of the products on sale

The shop is run by Vinod Sachdev whose father took over the business in November 2018. The family is from Afghanistan and came to England as refugees. They bought the shop from two Sikh brothers whose investment during 2018 transformed the former Costcutter store. Vinod's family are from a tiny Afghan Sikh minority.

The double front of the current building has only been that way since the late 1990s. Until then it had been two shops. Number 109 was an off-licence run by Jim and Maura Maloney, while number 107 was a sweet shop and newsagent called, at various times, Lanchbery's and New Bon Bon.

Despite the present and former shop(s) being entirely different, the market served is essentially the same. Drinks – Coca-Cola and Red Bull, vodka and cognac – are still at the core of the Nisa business, as are products for Graveney students.

Vinod's observation is that black people drink brandy and white people drink vodka. These include the local permanent and temporary Polish community, who make him smile. "Polish people don't care about money. They buy what they want – beers and groceries."
"When no 107 was called Lanchbery's, they had a vending machine outside selling chocolate. It wasn't good in the summer." [JR]

"Around 1980 the Bon-Bon sweet-shop and newsagent was taken over by Mr Patel and his wife, a very friendly couple who had a little boy. The latter went to Furzedown Primary School. Sadly, when he was five or six, he was killed in an accident on Nimrod Road and his parents were so distressed that they returned to India. *
"Local children would work as paper-boys and paper-girls for the Bon-Bon, delivering newspapers round the Furzedown area before going to school." [PG]

[*While several people confirm the Patels' loss, Arif Malida says the family left Furzedown for America, while Maura Maloney said that they moved to Canada.]

Sushil Avinash no longer lives in Furzedown. Or in the UK. In August 2019 he returned to his native Nepal to run a bar/restaurant in which he was already a sleeping partner. Having studied IT and Business Management at Reading University, he worked for the previous Sikh owners of Nisa at one of their other shops, in Eastbourne.

His plan is to develop a bespoke travel business based in his home city of Pokhara.

....

Jim and Maura Maloney took over the off-licence at no 109 on 1 July 1976 – a date Maura remembers well as it marked a particular stage in her pregnancy. "When we looked at coming, I said to Jim 'I can't live here, they're all old people'."

But the couple took the shop anyway, moved in to live upstairs – and ran it for 22 years.

At that time the off-licence was owned by Whitbread, though it had been empty for some time. As Whitbread changed its business model, the couple were able to buy the shop – which they did around 1984.

"But we left in 1998 because I didn't want to be there for another World Cup. During the previous one a group of rowdies from Stockwell had emptied the fridge and thrown out all of the ice-cream on to the pavement."

And it wasn't that all such incidents were caused by 'outsiders'. "Not long before we left, my husband was hit on the head with a bottle by a 'customer'. I'd had an attempted robbery at knife-point. And while working in the shop, my sister-in-law had been threatened with a machete. I had children and I didn't want the kids to lose their dad. Towards the end we always had three people working in the evening, because it was dangerous."

On top of that "it was just really, really hard, hard work. We were open seven days a week, from 9 in the morning till 10.30 at night. We were even open on Christmas Day."

And there was a constant threat from other people trying to get an alcohol licence, which would have profoundly damaged the business, and which Jim regularly opposed.

By the time they left, Maura says "I couldn't have done it any longer." And she feels that "We were lucky to get out of there alive."

James Maloney grew up living above the shop. "We used to have crisps and chocolate delivered to the door. I loved it."

111 Moyser Rd

1936 – United Dairies – dairymen
2019 – Café De Niro
Number of employees: 4

Café de Niro, with its beautiful art deco chromed fascia, was opened around 2002 by the former owner of the Kaptan dry cleaning business (at no 78). But since the end of 2018, it has been owned by Neset Sabir and his daughter.

Neset is from Turkey where he had been a policeman. He came to England in 1998 working at the Turkish Embassy. Three years later, he decided to leave the police and set up a business – making and selling pizzas.
"At that time my spoken English was ok but my English grammar was perfect because we had studied and studied it in Turkey. Now it's the other way round. I can speak English well, but grammar? Not so good." He also became a British citizen in 2009.

Running a small business in Furzedown is hard. Neset says that the turnover of the café is around £1750 a week, which provides precious little income from a working day that starts around 6 and finishes about 4. And the café is open seven days a week.

Despite the fact that Graveney pupils seem to love the place, he says that approximately 80% of the business' income comes from local building workers, with only 20% from local residents.
Q: Most popular dish on the menu? Full breakfast, and our home-made burgers
Q: Tea or coffee? 70% coffee. Freshly made coffee, £1 a cup. Only 30% tea.

Neset Sabir and his wife Hayriye are standing in the same place that the staff of Welford's Dairies stood when they were pictured almost 100 years ago. The entrance to the café now fronts Moyser Road. Originally the entrance was on the corner with Gracedale Road.

This picture of Welford's Dairies was taken in the early 1920s, before the shop had become United Dairies. At that time, being able to offer 'Absolutely Pure Milk' was quite a claim. Unpasteurised milk was, and remains, a source of transmission of tuberculosis from animals to humans. In the 1920s there was still no cure or treatment for TB.

The ex-launderette

Until the final quarter of the 20th century, the majority of UK households did not have 'all mod cons' – such as fridges and washing machines, or even telephones.

But, because most people can now conveniently wash clothes at home, launderettes are becoming an endangered species.

The Gibsons lived on Clairview Rd in the last of the bomb site new builds (no 28). She died 20 years ago, and her husband 15 years later. Their son Wayne was a local geezer with his white van, horse heads and trotting rigs. At Christmas his house was the wildest in Furzedown in terms of Santas and reindeer illuminations.

In December 2019, one of the most spectacular Christmas displays was at 11 Penwortham Road, shown above.

"The launderette on the corner of Gracedale Road was very busy and was run by Mrs Gibson for many years. It was a launderette until she died." [PG]

"The launderette was a very busy hub of activity and, like all launderettes, a place of varied smells and sights and queues and exchanges of chatter in a variety of accents and intonations and ways of speaking.

"The queues were of people wanting to use the small range of machines constantly in use, and for small change from the coin dispenser – when it worked.

"Sometimes one locally-based, machine-load-minder, man or woman, presided over all this activity and sometimes the service survived without that supervision – quite well.

"What sometimes seemed to matter most to small children, always with parent/s present, was the emptying of the very large, often hot driers after having watched their clothes tumbling through space – as though for ever."

"There was no rushing the time spent in the launderette, but once your washing was in – you could leave it – to take a welcome break, although before the days of Café de Nero, that would probably be back home." [GG]

"The launderette had big water tanks in the cellar, and the owner said that the cellar was haunted!" [JR]

Acknowledgements

First, we must thank the business people of Moyser Road who have been remarkably open and trusting of us as we have asked them questions and taken their pictures.

There have also been a number of local individuals who have contributed significantly to this project and have provided invaluable content. Some of it is acknowledged directly in the text, while some has become the background that provides a feel for the area and the guts of the story. In some cases they don't even know they have contributed. But I can't thank any of them enough.

John Brown: Streatham Society
Wendy Clarke [WC]: Florist at 72 Moyser Road
Sarah Forester [SF]: Nimrod Rd
Geoff Greensmith [GG]: moved to Furzedown in 1978
Peter Griffiths [PG]: moved to Gracedale Rd in 1977
Trevor Hutton [TH]: born in Beclands Rd in 1947
Helen Long: Local historian (Parklands Rd)
Arif Malida [AM]: founded Malida Accountants at no 66 Moyser Road
James Maloney [JM] son of **Maura Maloney [MMal]**. She ran the off licence at no 109 Moyser Road, and lives in Nimrod Rd.
Emrah Piro [EP]: Hairdresser at no 82 Moyser Road
Andrew and Jennifer Rolland [JR]: Jennifer's grandfather bought the Gracedale Road house that she lives in, in 1922.

Photographs

Most of the photographs in the book were taken by Alan Weller.
However, we have also benefited from the generosity of people with their photographs, and would like to thank in particular Jane TIngle (p2); John Brown and the Streatham Society (pp 15. 16 19, 25, 48 and 87) and Linda Lewis (p62).

And finally, of course, Arthur and Jane Tingle – without whom none of this would have happened.

www.ingramcontent.com/pod-product-compliance
Lightning Source LLC
LaVergne TN
LVHW072117070426
835510LV00003B/106